String, Donuts, Bubbles and Me

Favourite Philosophical Poems
By Wayne Visser

Second Edition

Second paperback edition published in 2016 by
Kaleidoscope Futures, London, UK.

First paperback edition published in 2014 by
Wayne Visser. First and second electronic
editions published in 2014 by Wayne Visser and
in 2016 by Kaleidoscope Futures.

Cover photography and design by Wayne Visser.
Cover photograph of the author by Indira
Kartallozi.

Printing and distribution by Lulu.com

ISBN 978-1-908875-28-0

Dedication

To my Dad, Berend Visser –
The philosopher of the family
Who is smarter than he believes
Wiser than he thinks
A teacher without knowing it
And a constant inspiration to me

Non-fiction books by Wayne Visser

Beyond Reasonable Greed

South Africa: Reasons to Believe

Corporate Citizenship in Africa

Business Frontiers

The A to Z of Corporate Social
Responsibility

Making A Difference

Landmarks for Sustainability

The Top 50 Sustainability Books

The World Guide to CSR

The Age of Responsibility

The Quest for Sustainable Business

Corporate Sustainability & Responsibility

CSR 2.0

Disrupting the Future

This is Tomorrow

Sustainable Frontiers

The CSR International Research
    Compendium

The World Guide to Sustainable Enterprise

About the Author

Wayne Visser was born in Zimbabwe and has lived most of his life in South Africa and the UK. He is a writer, academic, social entrepreneur, professional speaker and amateur artist.

Wayne finds the greatest teacher is life itself, which is given voice through this collection. His views on philosophy are best summed up in his own words:

> *Hanging by a golden thread*
> *Between the living and the dead*
> *Between beginning and the end*
> *Between a soul mate and a friend*

Wayne hosts a blog called Poets of Africa, where poets inspired by the great continent and its people can share their work.

Website: www.waynevisser.com

Email: wayne@waynevisser.com

Contents

String, Donuts, Bubbles and Me

According to scientists
The world's made of string
That buzzes and fuzzes
Or some such strange thing

It's also a donut
That curls round a hole
With middles and riddles
Just like a fish bowl

And there's no mistaking
It's more than 3-D
With twenty or plenty
Dimensions unseen

Still others insist
It's really a bubble
That's popping and bopping
Through the lenses of Hubble

Or is it just a big boom bang
That speeds to its goal
Of whirling and swirling
Into a black hole

My view is different:
The whole galaxy
Is milky and silky
And spins around *me*!

Cracked Pavements

The pavement blocks are neatly square
Yet sometimes cracks appear
That does not mean the ground we share
Will cave in to our fear

Our life is not a spreadsheet
Nor days like numbered cells
There is no sum when hearts meet
Nor code to break love spells

The branches of a tree diverge
The roots spread deep and wide
Yet water and sunlight converge
Like beaches and the tide.

Life's Dream

Life's a dream, it seems to me
In which we choose our destiny
We decide and we create
We walk the path and call it fate
And as we walk, we learn and grow
Until in time we finally know
That all is one and one is all
Here and now, forever more
If this is true, then let it be
That I wake to reality.

She: Light, He: Dark

In the dark, there is she
She is the light
In the light, there is he
He is the dark
Between the dark and the light
There is we
We the shade
We the place that light and dark
Has made

Night falls, she rises like a star
The dark welcomes she
Day breaks, he rises like a path
The light beckons he
Sunset, she passes
He flashes a smile
Sunrise, he passes
She blows a kiss

Then into the void, steps she

Against the voiceless silence

She cries

Amidst the heartless desert

She dies

So that others may speak

Be heard

So that others may breathe

Be free

Then into the sun, steps he

Under the glaring brightness

He sighs

Beneath the blinding whiteness

His guise

So that others may shine

Be seen

So that others may see

Be seers

She, our light, our passion flame

Sword of justice

Cleansing fire

Burning in the loveless night

He, our dark, our musing cloak

Pen of peril

Choking ash

Falling in the shameless day

Where darkness be

Let light become

And there is she

Where lightness be

Let dark befall

And there is he

She: light, he: dark

They pass, they touch

Together, they make shade

And that is how the world is made.

Un-doing

I know I can and yet I don't
I know I will and still I won't
It's in my hand, beyond my grasp
The future speaks of what is past
I know the when, the why and how
But what becomes of here and now?

What Dreams May Come

What dreams may come
What cosmos reflected
What masks may change
What seasons collected

We dance our love
We follow our vector
We flit our days
We gather our nectar

What dreams may come
What enchanted childness
What far horizon
What enraptured wildness

We roam our plains
We take our chances
We fix our gaze
We make our stances

What dreams may come

What earth-rooted treasures

What friends we make

What sky-varied pleasures

We find our pond

We quench our longing

We weave our spell

We let our soul sing

Quest Divine

A word, a phrase ... I catch my breath
Something stirs within my depth
Dancing flames to raging fire
All consuming soul desire

A glimpse, a hint ... my destination
Glowing embers, inspiration
Onward inward, still in mind
So much to do, so much to find

Now reflect ... seems out of reach
How am I this gap to breach?
Yet try I must, no price too fine
My holy grail, this quest divine

All the Clocks

All the clocks are running down
All our temples turn to dust
All the seasons wheel around
Say what you will, do what you must

The snowy peaks are set to thaw
Our high ideals will melt and drip
The streams become a waterfall
Erode our empires, bit by bit

All the clocks are running down
All our bridges turn to rust
All that's lost will yet be found
Lay down your bets on gods you trust

The battle's reached the castle wall
Our grand defence will never last
The pride of kings begets their fall
Our future echoes from the past

All the clocks are running down
All our dreams a bitter pill
All the cities sink and drown
Say what you must, do what you will

The ocean listens as we call
Our yearning drifts upon the tide
The planet wraps us in a ball
Our beauty soothes the fears we hide

All the clocks are running down
All our days are meant to thrill
All the fruits lie on the ground
So pick them up, enjoy your fill

The forest trees are growing tall
Our spirit reaches for the skies
The flowers bloom throughout it all
Our hope still blossoms on the rise

All the clocks are running down
All our rain and sun above
All the roads are nowhere bound
It matters not, if we have love.

Like Children

Like children in a play-pen
On and on we play
Telling our stories
Swapping our jig-saw pieces
Building and breaking our pictures
'Til slowly, slowly
Something beautiful begins to emerge
Something whole
Something ...

Wheel of Fate

We set the wheel of fate in motion
But cannot know the way it turns
We make the spark that lights a fire
But cannot know just how it burns

We are not masters of the weather
We are but sailors on the sea
We are not birds upon the feather
We are but hikers on the scree

We cast our gaze to the horizon
But never reach the shiny edge
We place each step upon the mountain
But never reach the rocky ledge

We are not pieces on a chess board
We are the player and the game
We are not someone else's picture
We are the painter – and life's our frame.

Casino Life

Some say that life's a gamble
In which you win or lose

You deal the deck
You place your bets
You hold your breath
And then collect your dues

But life is not all chance
Nor game of fight or flight
Sometimes the dice is blank
Sometimes the cards are white

Some say that life's a classroom
In which you live and learn

You make mistakes
You take your breaks
You grow your soul
And so the wheel turns

But life is not all graft
Nor school of tests and grades
Sometimes there are no lessons learned
Sometimes there are no accolades

Some say that life's a journey
In which you wend your way

You choose a path
You make your hearth
You walk your talk
And rise to meet the day

But life is not all quest
Nor march from A to B
Sometimes you move in circles
Sometimes you only dream.

Flame of the Spirit

Seminal spark

In the vast void of nothingness

Mighty devourer of darkness

Great warrior against eternal cold

Flickering flame

In the delusional shadow of a soulless
universe

Luminous beacon of our higher purpose

Gentle reminder of the divine in all life

Blazing fire

In the barren landscape of yesterday's
thinking

Passionate destroyer of perceived
limitations

Courageous torch of creative imagination

Smouldering ashes
In the healing breeze of tomorrow's dawn
Unifying essence of the ancient wisdom
Spawning nest of the Phoenix rising

Flame of the Spirit
In the tropical forest of life's diversity
Forever alight with faith, hope and love
Burn brightly within us, now and forever.

Castles

Castles built on sand soon crumble
Poems raised to love soon stumble
Lightning warns of pending thunder
Loss of heart's a kind of plunder

Harbours block out stormy weather
Anchors offer welcome tether
Broken vessels land in dry dock
Nesting eagles search for high rock

Stories need the grit of salt mines
Travellers need the light of star signs
Deserts need the cool of date palms
Journeys need the grail of love charms.

Tree of Life

Original seed
In the womb of mother earth
Germinated by a desire for meaning
Nurtured by the water of evolution

Founding roots
In the fiery lava of unconsciousness
Anchored by the principles of life
Thirsty for the mineral elements of
      sustenance

Tender tendrils
In the dark humus of creativity
Stretched towards the warmth of light
Called forth by the sky of destiny

Budding leaves
In the gentle rays of first knowledge
Turned to face the fire of passion
Tracking forever the sun of inspiration

Sturdy stem
In the changing winds of time
Joining our mother earth and father sky
Holder of the sap of wisdom

Spreading branches
In the varied seasons of the soul
Extended in the fellowship of love
Umbrella for the shadow of opposites

Succulent fruits
In the bountiful harvest of achievement
Fermenting new ideas under the moonlight
Spawning the seeds of the future

Exquisite flowers
In the colourful spectrum of rainbow spirit
Reflected in the stars of illumination
Unfolding the petals of enlightenment

Sacred symbol

In the harmonious voices of diverse
traditions

Dxui to the Bushmen, Simakade to the
Zulus

Kabala of the Jews, Eden of the Christians

Tree of Life

In the cosmic worlds of seen and unseen

Forever the inspired muse of creation

Connect us to the forest of the living whole.

Possibility

Could it be
Reality
Is not a lot of what
There is to see?

Is it true
That there's a clue
In rings and wings and things
Out of the blue?

What if skies
Before our eyes
Are bright with flight of light
That never dies?

What if trees
Sway in the breeze
And swoon and croon in tune
With hidden seas?

Is it true

That me and you

Each swirl and twirl and curl

With subtle hue?

Could it be

Eternity

Is not the plot of what

We choose to see?

Musings on Morphic Time

I. Measures of time

In ages past we have mapped the skies
Chartered its cycles
And plotted time against calendar and clock

Today we replace cogs with quartz
And tick-tock with digi-pulse
Surrounding ourselves with time fragments

We have tugged and teased the elastic of
     time
In our stretching towards the stars
Light years beyond our reach

We have sliced and diced the heartbeat of
     time
In our journeying inside the atom
Vibrating at femto-second pace

We have analysed time in our laboratories
As if by dissecting a butterfly
We can understand its beauty

II. Music of time

Time is a song
With interwoven sounds, rhythms and
    rhymes
Of harmony and discord

Humanity is deaf to the music of time
Fallen out of sync and out of tune
With the universal resonance

We have become slaves
To the hour, the quarter, the year
Chained to artificial time

We should be dancing to the beat
Of the moon, the generations, the living
    earth
Liberated by nature's time

Instead, we are dying

Poisoned by our selfish short-sightedness

But time will not blink an eye at our
passing

III. Masks of time

Time is a cruel slayer

When it destroys our youth, our hopes and
dreams

And reclaims our loved ones

Time is a kind benefactor

When it nurtures our wisdom, our
pleasures and passions

And fuels evolution in all life

Time is an impassive onlooker

When it observes our species, our
civilizations and planet

And sees cycles of birth and death

Time is a master magician

When it conjures our memories, our desires
and destinies

And tricks us into believing

Time is an innocent child

When it plays with building blocks of the
universe

And creates marvels of energy and light

IV. Masters of time

Our greatest power

Lies in the choices we make

About how we spend our time

Time is clay in our hands

For us to mould and manipulate, to shape
and sculpt

Into symbols of meaning

Time does not dictate to us
Whether to heal or harm, to love or hate
But time and karma are allies

Time smiles on concerted effort
Frowns on lazy expectations of entitlement
And rewards diligence and perseverance

Our greatest task
Lies in how we are able respond
To the gifts of time

V. Mysteries of time

Scientists and mystics rent the veil
On the temple of absolute time
Revealing a fourth dimension of relativity

Seers and prophets removed the mask
On the face of linear time
Gazing with equal clarity on past, present
        and future

Astronomers and imagineers opened the
   portal

On the matrix of time travel possibilities

Journeying through wormholes in space
   and mind

Yet many secrets remain

Held by time close to her breast

Until we are brave enough to call her bluff

Some say that God is eternal

That our destiny lies within a timeless
   realm

Only time will tell.

Life Scribes

A fresh sunrise
A blank white page
Where we as scribes
Record our days

Some words are wise
Some foolish too
We write our lines
By what we do

The lows and highs
Are traced with ink
Hellos, goodbyes
The thoughts we think

Time flits and flies
But not before
We note our lives
And play the score.

Real Magic

I know some real magicians
The living, laughing kind
Witches and wizards of life
If you know how to look, you'll find

The secret of their magic lore
Is to know what things can be
In every tiny acorn's core
They see a great oak tree

The spells they cast from day to day
Are proof of creation's worth
In every breath of liquid thought
They ensure the world's rebirth

The potions mixed in bubbling brew
Are ideas and ideals refined
In every active ingredient
They nourish the global mind

The wonders that they manifest
Are conjured from patient deeds
In every conscious act of will
They plant a bed of seeds

I know some real magicians
The living, laughing kind
Witches and wizards of life
If you know how to look, you'll find.

Song of the Star

What note am I? What transcendent tone
Which resonates in chords unknown
And reverberates in harmony –
An unseen cosmic symphony

What grain am I? What magic dust
Which congeals to form an earthy crust
Of mountain, valley, beach and plain –
An unseen cosmic soul terrain

What spark am I? What burst of light
Which dances over embers bright
And flickers flames of deep desire –
An unseen cosmic questing fire

I am nothing and all, the same and unique
The beginning I cherish, the end that I seek
I am mortal, eternal, nearby and far –
An unseen cosmic song of the star.

Synchronicity

Can you read the signs
Along the humming highways
Of our networked minds?

Can you see the reflections
In the meditative mirrors
Of our subtle connections?

Can you hear the musings
From the covert caves
Of our fated choosings?

Can you sense the complicity
In the overlapping orbits
Of our psycho-synchronicity?

Under-rated Pleasures

In life
There are
So many
Under-rated
Pleasures

Like waking up next to someone you love
And feeling the soft warmth of their body
The rise and fall of their reassuring breath
And the beating of their heart next to yours

There are
So many
Under-rated
Pleasures
In life

Like drifting between the worlds of
	dreaming and waking

When reality is still malleable as clay in
	your hands

When everything is possible and nothing
	forbidden

And the day's worries are as unreal as
	distant clouds

So many

Under-rated

Pleasures

In life

There are

Like seeing an elderly couple walking hand-
	in-hand

Still together and in love after all these
	years

Watching them smile at each other with
	affection

Or better still, *being* that elderly couple

Under-rated

Pleasures

In life

There are

So many

Like the joy of children playing without a
     care

Or the lilt of a busker's tune on a busy
     pavement

Like the sweet scent of a passing stranger

Or the wafted delights of food that makes
     you drool

Pleasures

In life

There are

So many

Under-rated

Like watching a robin bobbing outside your
window

Or listening to a cat purr when you stroke it

Like the boundless energy of a dog running
free

Or the tiny paws of a squirrel clutching its
nut-treasure

There are

In life

So many

Under-rated

Pleasures

Like the bliss of stepping into a hot bath or
shower

And the flicker of scented candles in the
dark

Like the flood of relief after you were
bursting to go

Or the buzz you get from a particularly
good sneeze

In life

There are

So many

Pleasures

Under-rated

Like the bouquet of a good wine on the
palette

Or a mature cheese that lingers in your
mouth

Like the surprising joy of pancakes in the
morning

Or the decadence of chocolate melting on
your tongue

There are

So many

Pleasures

Under-rated

In life

Like the voice of a friend on the other end of
    the line

Or a pillow-soft hug when you need it most

Like an unexpected kiss or a bunch of
    flowers

Or the wispy words of a poet in your ear

In life

There are

So many

Under-rated

Pleasures.

Riddle 1

What:

Keeps forever but is over in an instant?

Inspires loyalty but can lead to betrayal?

Speaks volumes but says not a word?

Signals greeting but bids fare thee well?

Scattered Books

I am single minded
Among my scattered books
And laser focused
Behind my fractured looks

I am neatly ordered
Beneath my messy papers
And purpose driven
Throughout my winding capers

I am quietly musing
Amidst the idle chatter
And always searching
For the words that matter

So judge not substance
By the mask of reason
Nor gauge true progress
By the whim of season.

Ghosts

We all have our ghosts –

Ethereal presences that linger in the
shadows

Of our sunny days

Ephemeral voices that whisper in the
stillness

Of our starry nights

Evanescent intuitions that flicker in the
iridescence

Of our lunar dreams

Ghosts of the past

Haunt the dungeons of our minds

Rattle the chains of our memories

And lure us ever backwards

Ghosts of the future

Tease us with visions of maybe

Taunt us with fairy tales of what-if

And tempt us ever forwards

Ghosts of death
Lurk in the quagmire of our anxieties
Summon doubts about our inimitability
And shroud our belief in the miraculous

Ghosts of life
Shimmer on the horizon of our being
Beckon to the promise of our divinity
And illuminate the potential of our love

Imagined ghosts
Are dreamed up to animate our voids
Conjured up to question our senses
And made up to justify our mass insanity

Real ghosts
Are discarnate souls and devic sprites
Angelic guides and demon ghouls
Forever infusing light and stoking fires

Malevolent ghosts
Are thirsty parasites that leech on our pain
Hungry predators that prey on our fears
And grim reapers that slay our hopes

Mischievous ghosts
Poke fun at our childish beliefs
Trip us up on our urgent treadmills
And drop enigmas into our rational mazes

Benevolent ghosts
Shelter us during tumultuous storms
Flash us with rainbow smiles
And raise us up above the illusory clouds

Mystical ghosts
Inspire our desire to live artfully
Tickle our curiosity to go beyond
And lift the veil on life's esoteric mysteries

We all have our ghosts –

Dancing phantoms that glide on the blurry
edges

Of our waking consciousness

Devouring spectres that feast on the
nourishing energies

Of our succulent present

Wistful apparitions that reflect the gods and
fiends

Of our innermost selves.

Confusion

Our confusion is the intrusion of illusion

Through the contortion of proportion

And the profusion in diffusion

Of the distortion of precaution

With infusion of our delusion in conclusion.

Ground Rules

Ground rules are the guidelines
Shouted from the side-lines
To make our wildness tame ...
As if life were just a game

Ground rules are echoes past
Lessons that are meant to last
To lead us through safe doors ...
As if life obeys our laws

Ground rules are our protection
From the fear of love's rejection
To give us places to hide ...
As if life can be denied

Ground rules are our choices
Whispered by inner voices
To keep our feet on track ...
As if life would turn it's back

Ground rules are habits worn
Like clothes since we were born
To curtail our whims and wishes ...
As if life were not capricious

Ground rules are the reply
Of those who cannot fly
To the beat of freedom's wing ...
As if life weren't born to sing.

Illusions

Our beliefs stretch as far as we take them
In our search for the purpose of living
And our faith is a mould that can shape
    them
In our lessons of loving and giving

But when streams become trapped we
    mistake them
For the limitless source of the ocean
In our quest for the gods, we forsake them
For the truth is in eternal motion

Our illusions are real as we make them
Like mirror tricks played with the sunlight
And our questions are hammers to break
    them
Bringing new worlds alive with our insight.

Riddle 2

What:

Holds tight as much as it lets go?

Unites two as much as it is bestowed by
one?

Gives back as much as it receives?

Serves the young as much as it comforts
the old?

Bits and Pieces

Hidden in drawers
Are pathways and doors
To mindscapes and heartshapes
And times long forgotten

Under the bed
Are words left unsaid
Like jars still unopened
And nest eggs unbroken

Stacked up in piles
Are papers and files
With thought-crimes and love-rhymes
And hopes now forsaken

Back of the shelf
Are bits of myself
Like gems left unguarded
And rags now discarded

Stashed in a box
Are keystones and locks
To histories and mysteries
And fates still encoded

Left on the floor
Are clothes from before
Like clues to unravel
And notes from soul-travel

Inside some books
Are triggers and hooks
To dark-nights and wing-flights
And trips still untaken

Strewn on the ledge
Are tales from the edge
Like sparks to enkindle
And memories that tingle

Flashed on the screen
Are photos and dreams
Of sun-bursts and moon-thirsts
And worlds yet untested

These are the bits
And though none of them fits
Each random played part
Turns my life into art.

Abbr.

midst techno-bustle
& market hustle
with email flurry
& retail hurry
brevity rules
among literary fools

memos whirl
& post-its swirl
msgs scuttle
& txts shuttle
by the letter
shorter's better

chatroom speaks
4 cyber-freaks
dumbing down
england's crown
with smiley faces
exchanging places

xtra time's

the modern crime

while humans race

thru' cluttered space

but life's too short

to just abort

subtle rhyme

& words sublime

find your voice

& make your choice:

to create

or to abbr.

Lost and Found

When I'm lost for words, I find my true
     voice
For silence is borne with the wisdom of
     choice
By finding my heart, I'm losing my head
For feelings are tangles of words best
     unsaid

When I've found myself, I lose my disguise
For freedom is built on the absence of lies
By losing my love, I'm finding my friends
For trusting begins when the certainty ends

When I'm lost in dreams, I find inner sight
For vision is masked by the spectrum of
     light
By finding my words, I'm losing my goal
For beauty is writ in the language of soul

When I've found my feet, I lose my desire

For purpose is fuelled by the passion of fire

By losing my way, I'm finding my path

For meaning is hid in the labyrinth's
      hearth.

Mirror, Mirror

Mirror, mirror, on the wall
Looking proud and standing tall
With twinkling eye and gleaming smile
Your charming face, sure to beguile

With tricks of light, you play your game
First you flatter, then you maim
A cruel master, seldom friend
Teasing, taunting, without end

Are you villain, evil glass?
A horror prop, or tragic farce?
Am I enslaved, or am I vain?
Will your spell drive me insane?

All alone, yet you conspire
With images of love's desire
Selling beauty, buying souls
Feeding fears and eating holes

You never lie, but miss the truth
By scorning age and praising youth
Catching beams, reflecting forms
Judging on distorted norms

Yet what you show is only part
Of who I am, it's just the start
The best of me is what you hide
It's all the beauty that's inside

Mirror, mirror, on the wall
I hear your voice and heed your call
The one you show is my true friend
You are the means, I am the end.

Angels

I believe in angels
But I don't think they have wings
I know that they are near
By the way my spirit sings

I believe in angels
But I doubt that they have halos
I know that they are wise
By the way their caring shows

I believe in angels
But I do not hear their hymns
I know that they are true
By the joy their presence brings

I believe in angels
But without the flowing robes
I know that they are here
By the light which shines and grows

I believe in angels
But not from realms of heaven
I know that they are close
By the loving that is given

I believe in angels
Some walk right by our side
Some dwell in planes unseen
And serve as spirit guides.

Wrapped in Words*

wrapped in words
and tied with rhyme
yet throughout space
not bound by time
enigmas fly

arched in rays
fade-marked with bows
resplendent land
in darkness glows
casts shadows on
archaic hope

masked in myth
encoded spells
reveal the quest -
lost legends live
in magic shells
narratives weave

- linked in light

twinned in tone
and making whole
opposites swirl

veiled in voice
in thought and deed
so hidden names
survive in seed
eternal words
recreate life

* Clue: acrostic

Heaven

Where is heaven?
Is it some place far
Or is it close
To where we are?

Religion cast
A seductive spell -
Go to heaven
Or straight to hell

But is heaven
A place in the sky
Or a fledgling soul
Learning to fly?

Heaven can be
A place on this earth
And so can hell
If we give it birth

Could heaven be
A state of mind
A way of being
For us all to find?

It is our right
To question why
But if we're wrong
I guess we'll fry.

Invisible

I am invisible, hidden, unseen
No one knows where I am, or where I've
    been
These moments pass by, alone, unshared
Nobody was there, nobody that cared

The fire of sunset, the swirl of cloudscapes
The swan on the river - the ripples it makes
The dance of lightening, the song of
    thunder
Alone I wander, alone I wonder

All this great beauty, the pain deep inside
With no one to tell, it's easy to hide
This they call freedom, living the dream
I am invisible, phantom, unseen.

Names

Names are tangled pathways to meaning
And secret tunnels to hidden treasure
Names are skeleton keys to sacred symbols
And enigmatic codes to scrambled
    messages

Names connect together
And affirm uniqueness
Names resonate with power
And quiver with subtlety
Names build bridges
And break down walls

Names are echoing voices of the past
And shimmering visions of the future
Names are the silky touch of the now
And the delicate breath of all eternity.

Space

Swirling with stars and galaxies
Pulsing with planets and nebulae
Asking questions without answers
Chasing beginnings without end
Echoing the distant song of creation

Sacred stories of our birth
Prophets' warnings of our death
Ancient myths of the heavens
Chartered maps of the skies
Eternally we quest for our place

Scattered light in the darkness
Puny warmth in the deep cold
Above and beyond yet also within
Calling us to stretch and explore
Explaining everything and nothing

Spawning the fiction of science
Playing with the props of matter
Acting on the stage of time
Casting the gods of destiny
Encore! for the cosmic drama

Sparkling with secrets and fantasies
Pregnant with the possibilities of life
Always there, yet never quite in reach
Creation swirls with order and chaos
Expressing our resonant inner worlds.

This is my Life

This is my life –

Like whispers in the trees
And swirling gusts of leaves
Like signal waves across the miles
And faces splashed with wistful smiles

Like flowers in the snow
And mushroom thoughts that grow
Like cosmic dust in empty space
And strangers gone without a trace

Like flotsam on the seas
And feathers on the breeze
Like scattered seeds on memory fields
And rainbow beads on battle shields

Like inkblots on the page
And birdsongs in a cage
Like reaching out into the void
And random acts of love enjoyed

- My life is this.

Poised

The pen, poised over a virgin page
The brush, held before a ghostly stage
The story of time scratched upon an age
The portrait of form framed within a cage

Without committing
All futures are possible
Before submitting
All bridges are crossable
No mountain too steep
No canyon too deep
No target to shoot for unmissable

The diver, toe-clinging to her board
The sailor, on his boat, harbour-moored
The lancer, slow, unsheathing her sword
The merchant, slick, conjuring his hoard

Without committing
No masterpiece can exist
Without submitting
No legacy can persist
No creations are designed
No revelations untwined
No love story starts with a kiss

We straddle the dream and the real
We join up the hub and the wheel
We spark the big bang in the nothingness
We play the sleight hand of our bluffingness

Each second that we move to choice
A silent world is given voice
Each moment that we choose to act
A crazy wish becomes a fact.

All Seems

All seems to spin
Now I lose, now I win
Now I'm sure, now I doubt
No way in, no way out

All seems to turn
Now I feel my insides churn
I feel no peace, I find no rest
Now my worst, now my best

All seems to drift
Now so close, now a rift
Now say yes, now say no
Nowhere to turn, nowhere to go

All seems to fade
Fleeting shadows, cloak of shade
Without within, this world of dreams
Life is never what it seems.

The High Wire

Can we dismantle a fortress from within?

Can we pour new essence into old wine-
skins?

At what point do our ideals become hollow
and self-serving?

When we don't sacrifice our comforts, are
we deserving?

Some days I feel like an act on the circus
high wire

Counter-balancing common sense actions
and irrational desires

I hear the echoes from my adolescence to
inspire:

"Constantly risking absurdity" and "a
hundred snowy horses unconfined"

I remind myself that I must walk amidst the
profanities

Of this world, but not be defined by them

I convince myself that I must honour
      responsibilities

Of daily life, but not be confined by them.

Invocation

May you always
Walk on the path of wisdom
Pluck the flower of healing
Dwell in the forest of meditation
And fly on the wings of love

For wisdom comes from walking
Healing is the blossoming of spirit
Meditation is unity with creation
And love cannot help but soar.

Wheel of Life

Wheel of life ever turning
Onward inward listening learning
Slowly quickly even pace
Backwards forwards face to face
Building up breaking down
Constant motion round and round
Circles cycles ebbs and flows
Ups and downs highs and lows
Beginnings endings old and new
Stop and think reflect review
Wheel of life ever turning
Onward inward listening learning.

Awake

The darkness comes, I close my eyes
Unknown void before me lies
Slowly it will crystallise
And take upon a dream disguise
Live the dream for soon it dies
Now awake, now open eyes
Awake once more and realise
Life's a dream, before we rise.

Ever?

Ever been amidst a crowd
And felt you were alone?
Or sensed somehow you were a stranger
Trying to get home?

Ever seemed you were an actor
Live upon the stage?
That all of life was but a drama
Words upon a page?

Ever stood aside yourself
And somehow had to smile?
For the one you were and the one you saw
Were strangers for a while?

Ever had the strangest feeling
Life was but a dream?
That any moment you would wake
To a wider reality?

If ever you have and thought it strange

Think it strange no more

Truth doth oft' disguise itself

In the hope that we'll explore.

Presence

Presence within me
I'm a seeker of your face
But as I turn my eyes inward
My thoughts and mind just seem to race

Still my mind, help me to focus
Still my mind, set me free
From the whirlwind that's inside of me
Oh, hear me, Presence within.

Y2K

The lure of nought, of nothing, of null -
To turn doomsayers' superstitions into self-
    fulfilling prophecies
To give fuel to fear and ego a bolder voice
To wage our wasteful wars on tiny turfs
To lose our self in the void

The power of circle, of cycle, of whole -
To mark endings in transition to new
    beginnings
To give life to hope and love another chance
To paint our dreams on a larger canvas
To find our place in eternity.

Spellbound

Countless clocks count down ...
Trapped in a time tied Hall of Mirrors,
We synchronise our beliefs
And accept the reality reflected

That a pointless point in time
On a superficial scale of history
Marks a new millennium
For all the people of the planet

Yet not so for the African Animist
The Judaist, or the Muslim
Neither followers of Confucius
The Buddha or Lao Tzu

Only those in religions self-absorbed -
Christian? Conservative? Corporate?
Only their narrow minds
By 2000 are spellbound.

Infusion

You infuse my mind -
With poignant truths
And reminders of harsh reality

You infuse my imagination -
With luring myths
And shadows of lives inspired

You infuse my heart -
With wrenching ache
And afterglow of "love and blessings"

You infuse my body -
With subtle inflections
And sense experiences relived

You infuse my vision -
With impish looks
And silver surfer's hair untamed

You infuse my breath -
With smoky scent
And soothing rhythm of conspiracy

You infuse my hearing -
With tinkling laughter
And sighs of too many burdens carried

You infuse my speech -
With turn of phrase
And attentive frown-mirrored listening

You infuse my writing -
With calligraphic care
And sacrifices of honest expression

You infuse my preaching -
With oversoul presence
And whispering echoes of inspiration

You infuse my emotion -

With jagged sadness

And thrilling precipices of glad expectation

In Memoriam: Bob Steyn

Caravan of Hope

They have no home
Other than the endless road
They know no life
Other than the restless journey
They have no friends
Other than the nomadic clan
They know no trade
Other than the merchants' way

Pre-dawn sees them strung out
Across the urban desert
Gathering disparate goods
For use and barter and sale
Blending effortlessly into their
      surroundings
Their passing goes unnoticed
Except by alert street guards
Who bark their respectful acknowledgement

These are the masters of survival
Living off the land
These are the teachers of solidarity
Sticking by their kin
These are the genii of commerce
Finding value in everything
These are the scholars of philosophy
Knowing life's worth

Oh, caravan of hope
May you discover oases
On your parched trail
May you reap rich rewards
From your creative enterprise
And may you one day lay aside
Your weary trolley load
And wonder no more
About the life of the unwanted
Wanderer.

Wish Upon a Star

One day I'll wish upon a star
And see you shining from afar
Gazing down from that high place
Winking with your twinkling face

I'll see your smile upon the sea
Reflecting on the moonlit beach
Dancing in the playful waves
Playing silly dolphins' games

And when the sun is setting low
I'll feel inside a soft warm glow
It is your love deep in my heart
Reminding me we'll never part

And when the sun is rising new
I'll see its rays and know it's true:
That night's not death, for every morn
The light shines bright, and life's reborn.

New Beginnings

Thank God for new beginnings
Forgiveness for past sinnings
The nightly balm of forgetting
On tender wounds of regretting
The daily reprieve of sunrise
From the dark shadows of reprise
Thank God for rejuvenation
The merciful rebirth of creation.

To Live Is To Have Tried

As you lie by my side
With your head on my chest
Our legs intertwined
My hand on your breast
The touch of your fingers
The smile on your face
The world is at peace
Everything's in its place

As the candlelight flickers
Our senses caressed
The music enfolds us
Safe snug in our nest
The cares of the world
Fade away without trace
We are cradled by love
In the soft arms of grace.

Private Lives

Today
My world is bright
I am celebrating long years of togetherness
In love

As I walk to the florist
My head is full
I am thinking warm thoughts of romance
In red

Just then
A funeral procession drives by
They are mourning a lifetime of loving
In black

With flowers they try
To beautify the ugliness of death
And recall a life that once blossomed then
        withered
In vain

Today

I am smiling while others are crying

I am in love while others are lonely

I am safe while others are threatened

I am content while others are hungry

I am living while others are dying

Tomorrow

Fortune's smile may turn to frown on my
    life

Black clouds may drift across the sun of my
    world

Love's bouquet may be exchanged for a
    wreath of sorrow

Tomorrow

I may have reason to cry

If I am suddenly alone, frightened and
    hungry

If love turns its back and hope deserts me

Then I too may wish for all the world

To die

This is life
And what can we do but live it
Grounded in where we are
Conscious of when we are
Truthful to who we are
Searching for why we are

For the world
Is never one place at any one time
And though we may share
Common experiences with many
Precious intimacy with some
Still we live private lives
Inside and out.

An Extra Ordinary Day

What would an ordinary day be like
If it was an extra ordinary day?
If at the very end of my life
I was given just one more sunrise and
    sunset
How would I spend that day?

Would I rush around like a man possessed
Grasping frantically at all those dreams
That were always on the horizon
But for lack of passion and daring
Never caught the tide and made it to shore?

Would I plan every precious marching
    minute
Trying desperately to fill in those gaps
That forever loomed like shadows
Cast by towering expectations and fears
Blocking the light of what might have been?

What if some wish-granting genie
Conjured another day with a lost love?
If we were united once more
For a single revolution of the earth
How would I share that day?

Would I make a long nostalgic list
Ticking faithfully through those favourite
    things
That never failed to make us smile
And returning to all those special places
Where we'd loved most deeply?

Would I write a poem of gushing words
Struggling vainly to say those important
    things
That got lost in the flood of feelings
And drowned in the eddies of pride
When we were together believing in forever?

How would I use another chance to grow

In the presence of my spiritual mentor?

If the teacher appeared once more

For a final round of esoteric lessons

How would I learn that day?

Would my mind be hungry with questions

Nibbling impatiently at life's succulent
mysteries

That tease my appetite like an enigmatic
riddle

And tangle my mind in a frustrating maze

Of endless dead-ends and unpredictable
turns?

Would I be an empty echoing vessel

Naively expecting to be filled with
fermenting answers

That would intoxicate my mundane world

And open the sealed vats of my
consciousness

To startling new perceptions of alternate
reality?

What would an ordinary day be like

If it was an extra ordinary day?

I can only hope that I would not squander

Such a sublime gift of time

In any of those ways I have imagined
possible

Rather I would wish for that day to be
ordinary

Unchanged in every way except this:

That I would be more aware more awake
more alive

With all my senses fully engaged

In every delicious moment of that extra
ordinary day.

Sometimes

Sometimes, we can only sigh
To express the way we feel
When our inner well is dry
And our wounds refuse to heal

Sometimes, we can only cry
To release the pain we hold
When our spirit starts to die
And we're left out in the cold

Sometimes, we can only scream
To unleash the rage inside
When our demons kill our dreams
And there's nowhere left to hide

Sometimes, we can only swear
To relieve the pent up stress
When our heart is full of despair
And our mind is all a mess

Sometimes, we can only breathe
To endure the choke of sadness
When our body aches to grieve
And our memories bring madness

Sometimes, we can only pray
To receive the strength we need
When our feet are shod with clay
And survival's our only creed.

Words

Words
Once spoken
Have a life of their own

Some words make history
Some are destined to change the future
Some words live forever
Some die almost as soon as they are born

As we breathe life
Into our words
Knowingly or unknowingly
We hope for the best

And yet sometimes
What we have spawned
Out of anger or pain
Is what we fear the most

For we create monsters

Who live an unnatural life

Turning dreams into nightmares

Leaving a trail of sadness

Some words cut deep

Some are the balm which can heal wounds

Some words echo truth

Some should never ever have been spoken

Words

Once spoken

Have a life of their own.

Sad Day

I never knew her
So why did it hurt to suddenly know
That she was gone?

Crushed beauty
Shattered youth
Sad day

I never met her
So why do I feel this aching space
Now she is dead?

Snuffed flame
Amputated life
Sad day

I never knew her
So why am I writing this poem
To remember her by?

Soulful eyes
Uplifting smile
Sad day.

Cry

Parched emotions
        Cracked and dry
A silent call
        A whispered reply
Rain pours down
        From molten sky

Exquisite beauty
        Beyond why
A way of being
        Naturally high
Discovering wings
        To stretch and fly

From the abyss
        An echoed sigh
The wrenching pain
        Of unthinkable goodbye
What to do
        But break down and cry.

Bridges

A bridge across time
Through music and rhyme
Crossing the wires
With flickered desires

A bridge across oceans
To mix magic potions
Seeing new sights
With sensual flights

A bridge across space
Where fantasies chase
Living our dreams
With nocturnal streams

A bridge across rivers
Where memory quivers
Recalling romance
And whirling rain dance

A bridge across forever
Held up by a feather
Joining our fates
As friends and soulmates.

T*B*L*F

Truth is the bedrock on which to build
Beauty is the shape of artful stone
Love is the roof of shimmering gild
Freedom is the choice to make a home.

Vortex

Spinning tops and turning wheels
Twirling dance and rhythmic reels
Churning waves and moon-spun tides
Whirling pools and dizzy rides

Rotor blades and tumble planes
Tempest moods and hurricanes
Magnet fields and milkshakes whirred
Spiral worlds and coffee stirred

Twisting rope and sunken wells
Cycle lives and woven spells
Swirling clouds and circle flight
Vortex love and spirits light.

Deep Thoughts

Deep thoughts and shallow fears
Begin with frowns and end in tears
Crushed hopes and shattered dreams
Destroy our faith in destinies

Deep thoughts and shallow needs
Souls that ache and hearts that bleed
Failed flight and poisoned past
Break promises meant to last

Deep thoughts and shallow rhymes
Recall the joy of magic times
Freedom's gain is truth's cost
But what is found if love is lost?

Sleepless Nights

For tortured days and sleepless nights
For darkened ways and faded lights
For bitter thoughts and acid rage
For words of blood scrawled on the page
For snuffing out the will to work
For demons that forever lurk
For all these things, I must be frank:
It's you and you alone I thank.

Friends

My life's encircled by my friends
A cherished ring that never ends

Some I've loved and others died
Some I've hurt and others lied
Some I'd take back if I could
Some I know are lost for good

It's friends that help me make it through
Those times I'm feeling sad and blue
And friends who share my happiness
When life's all joy and sunshine bliss

Many I have left behind
Many more I've still to find
Each one makes a choice to stay
Or they choose to walk away

It's friends that leave their special mark
Like candles burning in the dark

And friends who when we are apart
Are flames that burn within my heart

Some are old and ever dear
Some are far yet always near
Some are memories of the past
Some I hope will always last

The wheel of life never ends
And at its hub are my dear friends.

Lived Life True

What wise words can I give to you young
    one

As your precious life is scarcely begun?

Most of life's maxims you'll learn as you go

But still there are things I think you should
    know:

You'll love and be loved and so you will
    thrive

You'll hurt and be hurt and still you'll
    survive

You'll find and be found along your own
    track

You'll lose and be lost and make your way
    back

You'll look for answers and live your
    questions

You'll search for reasons and find your
    lessons

You'll cling to beliefs and learn to let go

You'll strive for freedom and reap what you
     sow

You'll have your hardships and fair share of
     pain

You'll earn your triumphs and squander
     your gain

You'll be downhearted and inspired to
     heights

You'll walk on the earth and dream of great
     flights

These few words of mine may not be all
     wise

But still they may help sort the truth from
     lies

So when you look back and your days are
     through

You'll have no regrets for you lived life true.

Though You Are Gone

Though you are gone
There still always
Will be:

An ache where once there was a glow
A pulse where once there was a beat
A sigh where once there was a kiss
A smile where once there was a laugh

My life moves on
But there always
Will be:

A spark where once there was a fire
A drop where once there was a storm
A blade where once there was a field
A grain where once there was a beach

I won't look back
But there always
Will be:

A word where once there was a poem
A note where once there was a song
A frame where once there was a scene
A flash where once there was a muse

My life is full
But there always
Will be:

A cloud where once there was a sky
A plume where once there was a bird
A ray where once there was a sun
A beam where once there was a moon

I look ahead
But there always
Will be:

A strand where once there was a rope
A stone where once there was a bridge
A tick where once there was a time
A spot where once there was a place

My life has changed
But there always
Will be:

A hush where once there was a sound
A thought where once there was a tale
A wisp where once there was a dream
A hope where once there a love

For you are gone
And yet remain
With me.

Wheel-Trap

The questions in the wheel-trap of my mind
Spin round and round like echoes without
    sound
The time-cogs of my memories slowly grind
Churning and yearning and re-treading
    ground

How could she do it? I have to know why
After all those years, to cheat and then lie
How could she do it? I thought that she
    cared
To show no respect, for all that we shared

The questions in the wheel-trap of my mind
Revolve like cycles in a vicious loop
The mantras that repeat, ensnare and bind
Will keep me jumping through the fiery
    hoop

How can I do it? I want to break free
From chains of anger that still shackle me

How can I do it? To now be a friend
For with no respect, it must surely end

The questions in the wheel-trap of my mind
Are riddles made to torture, tease and taunt
The answers are a key I'll never find
For phantoms always hover, hex and
        haunt.

Time Takes Its Toll

Time takes its toll ...

On dancing feet that start to plod
And willing hands that turn to clod
On sparkling eyes that dull from tears
And sprightly smiles that fade from years

Time takes it toll ...

When ahead is less than behind
Yet somehow still takes longer
When living is littered with dying
Yet gives no good reasons why
When memories we cherish fade
Yet those that hurt most remain

Time takes its toll ...

On flying dreams that crash and burn
And broken hearts that live and learn

On naive trust that's bruised and maimed
And primal hope that's caged and tamed

Time takes its toll ...

Complicated

Is it just me ...
Or does life get simpler
And love more complicated
The longer you live
And the more you love ...
Or is it just me?

Or maybe ...
It isn't life that gets simpler
But the simple things in life
That turn out to be more important
And that make life more worthwhile ...
Just maybe?

And perhaps ...
It isn't love that gets complicated
But me who has become more complex
Who is now more interesting
And who is more difficult ...
Just perhaps?

Is it just me ...

Or does love get deeper

And life more superficial

The longer you love and

And the more you live ...

Or is it just me?

Stone in My Shoe

You're the surf in my tide
The thorn in my side
The buoy when I sink
And the spike in my drink

You're the pearl in my clam
The flaw in my plan
The lift in my wings
And the knot in my strings

You're the fire in my flue
The stone in my shoe
The knife in my back
And the gold in my sack

You're the hole in my pale
The wind in my sail
The crease in my frown
And the jewel in my crown

You're the storm in my sky

The glint in my eye

The end of my rest

And the grail of my quest.

Friends Are Like Mirrors

Friends are like mirrors
In which are reflected
Our face without masks
And our memories collected
They let us see clearly
The treasures we've hidden
The choices we've made
And our destiny bidden.

We Could

We could …
But what about consequences?

I've thought about it
And savoured the thought
Dreamed about it
And woke up still smiling

So, we could …
But what about responsibilities?

The thrill of beginnings
Leads to the ache of endings
Happy-go-lucky now
Means sad-and-lonely later

Yes, we could …
But what about expectations?

I've danced with images
And felt the beat of anticipation
Sung the very scenery
And heard nature join the chorus

No doubt, we could ...
But what about destinations?

The paths of travellers
Cross, tangle and part ways
The stars of destiny
Seldom blink and shine in sync

We could ...
But would we? And should we?

One True Light

The world shook
And I felt the tremor
Fires raged in the City
While my flame died

Battered
Beaten
Broken

I rose from cinder
Turned my back
To smoking sky
And walked away

Barefoot
Bruised
Blistered

I walked on pebbles
Forward step by step

Towards the barricade
And a new harbour

Warmth
Light
Rest

I found respite
A safe place
Storm protected
Calm and cosy

Seagulls
Salt-air
Surf

I hear wilderness calling
Cut the moorings
Drift out to sea
Dance with the wind

Wink
Blink
Think

I recognise the beam
The searching signal
Land ahoy!
My one true light.

No War!

Don't speak to me of holy wars
Of martyrdom and sacrifice
Don't speak of an enlightened cause
Of infidels and paradise

There is no decent way to kill
No comfort for a widowed bride
There is no vengeful divine will
No godly plan for genocide

Don't speak to me of hidden bombs
Of dictators and liberty
Don't speak of righting nations' wrongs
Of winning peace and setting free

There is no gold that's worth a life
No oil that's worth the blood
There is no diamond worth the strife
Of sordid profits from the mud

Don't speak to me of sacred ground
Of ancient consecrated earth
Don't speak of treasures lost and found
Of claiming back His place of birth

There is no faith that teaches hate
No doctrine founded on revenge
There is no violent seal of fate
No prayer to make the bloodshed end

Don't speak to me of wars for peace
Of battles for the hearts and minds
Don't speak of blames that never cease
Of hurt that heals and pain that binds

There is no glory in a war
No victory in futures lost
There is no flag worth killing for
No profit that can match the cost.

Secret of Success

You say you want to know (and others too)
The shining secret of my life's success;
My ten-step, rags-to-riches recipe
And my ascendant path to happiness.

Do you mean the grail of heroes' quest?
Is that the secret you were hoping for?
Tales of dreaming big and acting boldly;
Of stumbling upon fortune's golden door?

Alas, the hidden truth (invisible
Behind the bright myth of a master plan)
Is that, no sooner is the mask removed,
Than cracks appear in the sun-bronzed
      tan.

My dark secret is that things fall apart
Almost nightly in the shadows of fame,
When the glaring spotlights of intrigue fade
And fragile self-esteem crumbles to shame.

My hushed secret is that the booming voice
Becomes a gnawing whisper of self-doubt
In the echoing caves of solitude;
An endless maze where only demons shout.

My small secret is that the starlit rise
Shines bright against a black, black empty
    sky;
And even as the peacock struts its plumes,
Its wings are clipped short and it cannot fly.

The secret of my success ... is failure
(If you, and others too, still want to know);
It's scrambling across the yawning chasm
Between where I am and where I must go.

It's waking up hungry for self-respect
And going to bed thirsty for respite
From the chattering voices in my head
That tease with vivid dreams of flight.

It's stretching and striving and surviving
The onslaught of seeing the potential

At the edges of my unsettled state
Of relentless angst that's existential.

It's throwing a rope across the river
Daily, between what is and what could be;
It's showing the world, not the best I've got,
But the best bits I want them to see.

To succeed in life is to fail and fail
And still keep giving more than you can
        take.
My secret of success, since you *did* ask,
Is to know what's real from all that is fake.

Yesterday, Today, Tomorrow

Yesterday
I was muddled and cuddled and bubbled,
Living brightly and lightly and spritely;
But the world turns,
The flame burns,
The mill churns
And yesterday is gone.

Today
I am weary and bleary and teary,
Feeling tired and mired and uninspired;
But the world spins,
The sail trims,
The spade wins
And today will pass.

Tomorrow
I may be sunny or funny or crummy,
Having mopped up, or topped up, or cocked
        up;

So the world wheels,

The past heals,

The mind reels

And tomorrow will come.

Yesterday, today, tomorrow:

With love or loss, with joy or sorrow,

Like waves to ride, seasons and tides;

We take the test,

We do our best,

In life's great fest

While the world whirls.

The Edge

The world is round
Until we walk right off the edge
Our lives are poised
Forever teetering on a ledge

Endless circles
Round and round
Until it stops
Without a sound

The world is round
A perfect, spinning, sparkling sphere
Our lives are strung
Stitched up with love and glued with fear

Unravelling
Start to end
We fall apart
We lose a friend

The world is round
But it may just as well be flat
Our lives are linked
Forever breaching this and that

No matter what
We reap behind
What counts is how
We sowed our time.

Message in a Bottle

These crumpled words adrift in time
At sea on waves of bottled rhyme
My message to an unborn child
An island echo from the wild

Beware of those who claim the truth
Who always speak with certainty
Embrace the dreams of hopeful youth
But don't get lost in fantasy

Stay clear of those who feed the grey
Who only praise the dutiful
Rejoice in random acts of play
And treasure all that's beautiful

Stand up for those who would be free
Who only need a chance to shine
Oppose all forms of slavery
Especially thoughts that chain the mind

Look up to those who serve to lead
Who nurture buds and water shoots
Find love and tend it like a seed
That takes its time to put down roots

These bottled words, uncorked at last
Imbued with wishes from the past
A phantom speech upon the shore
My invitation to explore.

#socialMEdia

Tell me, do you Like me?
Please answer quick, I've got to know
Are we Friends forever?
'Cos if we don't click, you'll have to go

Did you just Accept me?
Feel free to Browse my latest hols
And did you see my Status?
I'm sure we'll Share a bunch of lols

Do you want to Follow me?
Monitor my E-heartbeat
And can I be your Favourite?
Be sure to hashtag and Retweet

Shall we get on LinkedIn soon?
I'm hoping you will Digg my stuff
Or otherwise, just Tag me?
I'll never call your Online bluff

Did you see my Album?
I've Pinned my wall with favourite pics
And did you watch my Channel?
I'm Posting loads so something sticks

But tell me, don't I know you?
It feels somehow somewhere we've met
An avatar like yours?
It's not a face I'd soon forget.

What Lies Beneath

You see me –

and seeing, you think that you know me.

But you do not know me,

any more than you know the mysteries of a
    galaxy

from seeing its image projected on a screen.

What you see is not an illusion,

but neither is it the full picture –

for it lacks colour, and depth, and
    movement.

What you see is a dull facsimile of me,

a spark of fire extinguished to grey ash

in the act of capture.

For I am so much more than you see –

and also so much less.

I walk around with a hurricane of thoughts

swirling and flashing in my head;

yet not a single hair

will you see out of place.

I climb and swoop across skies of ecstasy,

gliding on wings of beauty;

yet all the world will see

is the steady plod of my feet.

I stumble blindly in tunnel mazes

of grief and self-loathing;

yet I will greet you with a smile

on my sad-clown face.

I radiate with love so bright

that I must have swallowed a supernova;

yet the world will never be scorched

by the sun of my desire.

You hear me –

and hearing, you believe that you
        understand me.

But you do not understand me,

any more than you understand the secrets
    of elephants
from listening to the trembling air.

What you hear is not a lie,
but neither is it the whole truth –
for it lacks history, and nuance, and
    narrative.
What you hear is a distant echo of me,
a burst of song faded to a faint pulse
in the moment of listening.

For I am so much more than you hear –
and also so much less.

I weave stories so enchanting
they would leave generations spellbound;
yet you are treated only to the silence
of my vellum-bound heart.

I ache with pain so buried
that screams cannot penetrate the abyss;

yet the world will never eavesdrop
on the black well of my loss.

I sing melodies that spontaneously erupt
into a million iridescent butterflies;
yet you will not sense even a flap
of those winking wings.

I translate the noisy babble of nonsense
into sacred books of wisdom;
yet the world will never whisper the words
on the pages of my soul.

You see me –
but if you would know me,
only look in the mirror.
For your covert storms and boundless
        firmament,
your dark tunnels and explosive love –
these are a truer reflection of me
than the mask I wear for all the world
(and you) to see.

You hear me –

but if you would understand me,

only listen to your heart's song.

For your magic spells and silent screams,

your winged symphonies and wise
      parchments –

these are a clearer intonation of me

than the script I voice for all the world

(and you) to hear.